Tackle Squash

Tackle Squash

Jonah Barrington
with John Hopkins

Stanley Paul, London

Also by Jonah Barrington

Barrington on Squash

Stanley Paul & Co Ltd
3 Fitzroy Square London W1

An imprint of the Hutchinson Publishing
Group

London Melbourne Sydney Auckland
Wellington Johannesburg and agencies
throughout the world

First published 1976
© Jonah Barrington 1976
Illustrations © Stanley Paul & Co Ltd
1976

Set in Monotype Times and Univers

Printed in Great Britain by litho by
The Anchor Press Ltd, and bound by
Wm Brendon & Son Ltd
both of Tiptree, Essex

ISBN 0 09 127880 5 (cased)
ISBN 0 09 127881 3 (paperback)

Contents

Introduction

It would be a happy coincidence if we could recall here that the idea for this book came to myself and my collaborator John Hopkins instantaneously, striking us like a thunderbolt as we pursued our various paths; I, in my daily preparation for the British Open. John in search of another story for his newspaper.

We can't. The idea came to us jointly borne high on a silver plate by Roddy Bloomfield, a publisher whose experience with similar tennis books convinced him that there was a successful market for just such a book on squash.

The pith of this book, its very heart, is in the sequence of photographs which, when flicked at speed, show me illustrating how to play a stroke, be it forehand or a drop or a backhand volley, from beginning to end. No other book that we know of presents what we hope to be the correct way to play the stroke so simply and vividly. Don't know where to put your left foot on the forehand drop shot? Should you wave your right hand around as you go in to pick up a low volley? The answer is simple. Look it up.

This is a book showing not immutable bronzed men, muscles flexed, in statuesquely correct positions. It is a book that shows me moving around the court. There is more life in the pictures than in most squash instructional pictures because they were shot as I played the stroke in question. My head bobs, my brow furrows; exactly what happens in a match or game. The camera doesn't lie. Not often at any rate. So what you see before you is me for better or worse and most of the time I hope for the better.

We have tried to show orthodoxy in each sequence but squash is a game of vicious movements, of leaps and darts and lunges, and the flicker sequence will thus show occasional variances from the classic positions. We don't mind that because we wanted realism. Of course, the best technical players such as Ken Hiscoe might make perfect models. Despite being 6 feet tall and a hefty $12\frac{1}{2}$ stone, he pads around the court stealthily and still gets lower to the ball than most. But don't forget that 30% or 40% of the other top players regularly hit the ball off the wrong foot. And even Ken Hiscoe transgresses from time to time.

In some of the flicker photographs and in photographs in other sections of the book you will also catch a glimpse of another person in the background. This is my collaborator John Hopkins and we hope that his presence will add credence to our claim that this is a realistic book. Too many books in our experience tend to show only one player, who is inevitably the demonstrator, and him in the ideal position on court. They tend to forget that very often neither player can get anywhere near the ideal position on court and thus they lose their validity.

The inclusion of John, a good club player, is meant to help relate what I am saying to players of his standard. It is very easy for the top professionals to see their own problems clearly but to forget that these are not the same problems that club players and even beginners face. After all, what is simple for the professional is often difficult or even impossible for lesser men. We have tried to make a marriage of the two by using me as an example for those aspiring to better things and John as an example of someone who plays only for fun and, consequently, hasn't the time to spend on his game rubbing out the kinks that have grown into his playing style over the years.

If you are particularly hawk-eyed you will notice in some of the photographs that John's grip is incorrect. It is like an axe-man's. He is holding an £18, delicately balanced, gut-strung instrument as if it was a £2 Woolworth's meat axe.

He is not alone in this failing either. I dare say that the majority of club players hold the racket incorrectly. I won two British Opens with a grip of dubious parentage and then I realized that it was wrong, put myself through an agonizing three months changing my ways and finally settled for the grip on page 17.

My noble collaborator is not up to scratch in other ways, too. A tall, lean man, he doesn't bend his knees enough to get down to the ball as Hiscoe does for instance. He stretches to play his shots instead of moving forward another half pace where he would be able to hit the ball more comfortably and, probably, more powerfully. However, for the sake of realism, we have made no attempt to conceal these faults.

As I said earlier, our aim throughout was to produce a book that would appeal both to beginners and the better players. From the questions put to me when I give clinics I know that people want to know the right way to play squash. I also understand that given the limitations of being amateurs and thus having to work for a living, many club players don't want to remodel their game. They want to be advised of ways of making minor modifications that will bring major improvements. As part-time players they have every right to look for such tips.

I hope that in this book we will go some way towards helping them. I also hope that we have created a sense of movement in the flicker pictures and that the readers will be grateful to us for sparing them yet another museum-like display of inanimate photographs.

Significant changes in the Rules were made in 1976, and they came into effect on 1st January 1977. Many of the controversial Rules have been completely re-written and the interpretation is now simple. You should, however, read them closely and they are included in chapter 10 of this book.

1. Equipment

If you were a beginner, John, I would recommend you to buy specialist squash clothing rather than tennis clothing. Squash kit is purpose built, so to speak, which means the trousers are designed not to split when you stretch for a drop shot. Often, too, they are easily washable.

As I say, if you were a beginner I would also suggest that you don't go out and blow £10 to £15 on making yourself sartorially in the First Division when your game is in the Fourth Division. If you want to then do so by all means. I am merely saying it is not necessary to do so. Just remember: the Squash Rackets Association insist that clothing should be all-white or that the majority should be white. That means that however much you may be attached to your stripey old rugger socks and your old red rugger shirt they won't be allowed on court.

There is a good reason for this rule. It is easier to follow the flight of a black ball if it contrasts strongly with one's clothing as well as the colour of the court. And if you wear old tennis or boating shoes then their coloured soles may well leave scuff marks on the floor of the court, which make it hard to see the ball on the floor. This is the worst offence of all,

I think, because the floor of a brand new court can be ruined within a few months if people persist in wearing shoes with black, brown or any marking sole.

That is general advice. Now let me be specific. First shirts. The better squash shirts will stretch, are long enough to tuck into a pair of shorts and sometimes have different coloured collars. But plain, simple T-shirts,which are probably cheaper, are fine to start with. The same with shorts. You can get pairs with pockets or with a strip of towelling down each side for you to wipe your sweaty hands on. You can also buy perfectly acceptable pairs that do not have pockets or towelling strips and so cost less.

Nowadays there are squash socks that have thicker soles, often referred to as cushion soles, to help protect your feet from the bashing you are about to give them on court. They can be cotton and wool, wool and nylon, almost any mixture or not a mixture at all. It's every man for himself here. I can't advise other than to say that I wear one pair of woollen stretch socks. My feet are so hard now that socks don't give me much protection. In my case they are more aesthetic than functional.

There are specialist squash shoes available now. It is no longer necessary,

13

nor particularly advisable in my view, to buy tennis shoes. They will tend to have too soft uppers that might stretch or even tear after a while. Furthermore, they don't give such good support to the feet as do sturdy squash shoes that are also designed to help grip on a wooden floor of a squash court and not a grass or hard tennis court surface. If the shoes don't fit perfectly then don't be afraid to put on another pair of socks. The important thing is to make sure your feet don't slide inside the shoes. If they do you will have blisters on your feet and you might break a few toenails as well.

In general the thing to remember when you buy clothes is to make sure that they are comfortable. The first time you play you don't have to look as if you have just stepped out of the best sports outfitters in town.

You will need a ball but the precise sort depends on whether you play on hot or cold courts. A rough guide is that the colder the courts the bouncier the ball you need. There are four types of ball all indicated by a coloured dot stamped on the ball: a yellow dot is the slowest, the type used in championships; a blue dot is the fastest and balls stamped with a red or a white dot are in between a blue and a yellow. As a beginner don't be afraid to use a white, red or even blue ball to

14

make sure you get a rally going. Squash is hard enough without making it even harder by playing – or trying to play – with a ball that won't bounce.

Lastly a racket. The most important piece of equipment that you will buy and probably the most expensive. My advice is to buy a good strong one to start with, bearing in mind that from time to time you will accidentally swipe it against a wall. It would be a tragedy to break an £18 racket by hitting it on a side wall. It is not necessary for it to have gut stringing – the best kind in other words. Synthetic stringing is perfectly adequate and much cheaper. I prefer a wooden-shafted racket because the wooden shaft gives me more feel of the ball on the racket head. As for a grip, I suggest you find one that is comfortable. A leather grip is inclined to become slippery after a while. I prefer a towelling grip, which is what is fitted to most rackets anyway nowadays. Towelling absorbs sweat well.

2. The Grip

I won a number of British Open championships with what I now call an incorrect grip. It took me three months
to change it. If you can learn to hold the
racket correctly then it should be easier
for you to hit the ball correctly. A simple
guide is to place the head of a racket in
your left hand and offer the handle to
your right hand, assuming you are right-
handed. If you are like me a left-hander,
then to your left hand. Shake hands with
the racket handle and your hand will
then be in, more or less, the correct
position.

It is essential that the forefinger grips
the racket handle outside the thumb and
that it is not restricted inside the thumb
with the three other fingers. The forefinger in this trigger position helps to
maintain the balance of the racket.

Keep the palm of the racket in the
heel of your hand, though I don't mind
if occasionally you move your hand
further up the shaft for a delicate drop
shot. The correct grip with the forefinger
extended will naturally be of the right
strength; you won't have to grip any
tighter or looser.

Most of all, be comfortable. There
are good players with bad grips just as
there are bad players with good grips. I

want you to become a better player and
I suspect that this may mean improving
your grip.

The grip on the left is wrong. The
index finger is too close to the
middle finger. Note how the grip on
the right shows the index finger
curled as if around a trigger.

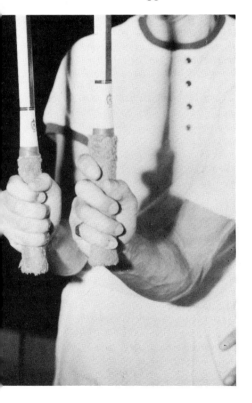

3. The Basic Strokes

FOREHAND DRIVE

The emphasis is on the footwork and the rotation of the body so that even up to impact the player retains the choice of a number of strokes–a drive, a boast for instance, even a cross-court drive. As I move to the back left-hand corner so my racket is coming up. Note how I go down, 1 to 5, to get the ball out of the corner. Notice that I put my left foot into the corner first, not, as purists maintain I should, my right foot. I believe, and so do Geoff Hunt and other

1

18

FOREHAND DROP

2

FOREHAND VOLLEY

FOREHAND BOAST

3

19

FOREHAND DRIVE

4

5

20

leading players, that when one is going into the forehand back corner it is essential that one leads with the wrong foot in order to make it easier and quicker to get out of the corner again. If I put my right foot into the corner first then I would probably only be able to to play one stroke and that would be a boast. I don't think I would be able to swing around to play a drive. I have now pivoted and I am swinging out of the corner in 6. The racket has some through and away and I am carried through with the momentum towards the centre of the court. There is immense attention to the cocking of the wrist, the

6

bending of the legs, keeping the head down for that fraction after the completion of the stroke. That rotation out of the corner is very important. If you don't do it you will be trapped in the back corner unable to move. I play the stroke and go with it. If I had swung my left shoulder further around I would have had great difficulty in controlling the ball down the wall. The movement of the shoulder and body in the pivot must be rhythmical, not jerky.

22

BACKHAND DRIVE

I am advancing on the ball and preparing to play the stroke. I am not completely upright, 7. There is an emphasis on footwork. My intention is to strike the ball with the left foot forward and the right foot behind and to do so with as comfortable a stride as possible. I am getting the racket back and this is very clear-cut in the pictures just before impact. As I move in on the ball my racket goes through a movement that you could almost call a Geoff Hunt twirl though it is at a different angle. I am stretching right into the ball, 8, and taking a long stride. I am not going through too tight

7

8

to the body and as I swing notice that
my feet are basically pointed towards
the corner of the court. Because I am
going forwards I am able to open my
shoulders a little more than I would if
I was closer to my opponent and at the
same time notice that I have not swung
my right shoulder around. Notice how
high the racket travels, 9. There is
good freedom of stroke, good depth to
the drive, good bending of the knees,
balance, head down, the right shoulder
down, not lifting the head too soon. As
I complete the stroke and start to move
back to the centre of the court notice
that the racket head is up and I am turn-

24

9

10

11

ing my body around, 10. Notice also the emphasis I place on getting into a spring position when I have finished the stroke, 11. The wrist is cocked, which means the racket head is in a position where I can bring it up to the forehand or backhand ready for the next stroke, should there be one. From the beginning the eyes have been following the ball.

FOREHAND VOLLEY

I am just behind the centre of the court. I have followed the course of the ball through and as I have assessed what it is doing so I am starting to move to the left

26

with the racket in position. I am moving forward. I am not upright but neither am I crouching. I am in a position from which I can spring. Notice how closely my eyes are watching the approaching ball and the way in which the racket first goes back for preparation of the stroke, 12, and then the face of the racket gradually opens, 13, 14, 15, 16, so that at impact I will slice the ball and I therefore control it more decisively. I have my head down over the ball and I am aiming to hit it on to the front wall as low as I dare and as near to the side wall nick as I dare. My stride into the ball is quite long, 16, yet remains steady. My right arm is thrust

12

27

13

14

28

15

16

29

17

out and used to help me maintain balance. It doesn't dangle by the side of my body. Notice how the left elbow remains bent at impact, 17, and thereafter while the racket goes through and then up the wrist remains almost totally cocked throughout. After impact notice I am not overbalancing. As I watch the ball I am travelling back towards the centre of the court.

BACKHAND VOLLEY

I am poised just behind the T. This is a good position. I am crouched, ready to spring and the racket is in a position so

30

18

that I can move it from one side to the other, 18. Note how in 19 I am starting to draw my racket back. It is very apparent that I am going to have to go upwards towards the ball and in 20 I am beginning to stretch out. Again there is this attention to detail, watching the ball, keeping the racket head up, stretching across. It is essential not to overbalance on this stroke. They say volley at all costs. I don't entirely agree. Volley providing you can volley to a purpose. If you are going to stretch across, bury your knees and your nose in the wall, then it would be better to let the ball go to the back of

31

19

the court and dig it out from there. Having watched the ball I am coming on to it. Notice I have bent my legs. I am not arriving at the ball in a martial position. I am almost going off the ground, 22, though that doesn't happen too often. On 21 I am getting my racket back stretching upwards across court. You can see the legs working on this one. The stretch remains controlled throughout. Notice that I am up on my toes and from then on I am fully extended without taking off. The limit of my stroke can be seen on 23. I seem to have a lot more flexibility and I could be playing two types of volley. I

32

20

could be playing deep down the wall or I could be playing a short kill. I've got the racket right back, especially in 21 – it's almost sloping down on a line through my shoulders down to the floor. Then I start bringing it through again with a cocked wrist and taking it wide, 22. Notice that the wrist does not break, that the arm almost straightens at impact, 24, and not before. Notice the balance. I've gone for a short kill in the front of the court and I haven't accepted that the ball is going to be a winner and I'm balanced ready to play another shot should it happen. The racket face is slightly open at contact.

21

22

34

23

24

FOREHAND BOAST

My dreaded opponent has played a backhand stroke down the wall but the ball is running short and not to a length. I am coming forwards from behind the T, assessing the possibilities and with my opponent trapped behind me in the backhand corner, 25, I decide to play a forehand boast that will take the ball and my opponent to his front forehand corner, making him run diagonally across court. In 26, I have trailed the racket head well back to keep my opponent guessing. Although I am square to the side wall it is not until 27, which is impact, that I reveal my true intentions. He only begins to

25

26

27

move at the time I make impact, which leaves him precious little time to cover the length of the court. The angle of my body to the side wall has allowed me to angle the ball and the racket has followed through on the line of the body as well and is slightly open at impact. I have sliced the ball into the side wall, which gives me more control, though many players favour a flat, hard-hit stroke with less margin of error. As the ball moves to the far corner my body gradually swings around, the racket remains well up, the wrist is cocked and I can easily take the centre of the court. Throughout the stroke I have maintained the initiative forcing him to scamper furiously from back to front. That is a situation I like.

BACKHAND BOAST

This is a very rhythmical stroke. It is essential for me as a left-hander that I don't plant my foot deep into the corner of the court and am then unable to turn on it. If I am going to play this boast I have to make sure I have got my feet positioned so I can swivel out of the corner, coming out, in effect, with the ball. An ideal time to play a backhand boast is when my opponent has overhit the ball and it is coming off the back wall. As I go back to play it, notice how I get the racket head

38

28

up and back, 28, so that I arrive at the ball ready to play a stroke. As I go back into the corner I am bending both my back and my legs. When I have got my balance and I start to swivel, 29, notice the racket head is right up. You see the body starting to move behind the ball. In 30, I am still taking the weight on my right foot but from 31 to 34 (through the course of the stroke) I transfer my weight on to my left foot, and because of this comfortable turn I am in a good position to follow the course of the ball and move easily back to the centre of the court. This boast is hit firmly and

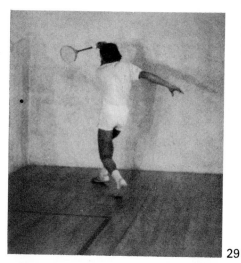

29

30

40

31

32

41

33

34

42

almost flat. I am helped in moving off the stroke by the way I have put my right foot into the corner and also by allowing the racket head to swing through and, so to speak, lead me back to the centre of the court (34).

FOREHAND DROP

I have moved off the T as I have sensed that the ball is going short. I have my racket right back again, 35, and I have my eyes trained on the ball assessing exactly where it is going. I am gradually going down to the ball and for this shot I am going to have to bend very low and

35

bend my back. I want to play the ball no more than two or three inches above the tin and therefore I have to get everything right. I must play the ball in an orthodox manner. If I play it off the wrong foot then I am likely to be penalized because I can't get out of the way in time. I concentrate on the ball and not on what my opponent is doing behind me. Notice in frames 36 to 41, that I come down with no wavering of the racket head and that the racket is open because I am going to slice the ball to take pace off it. I am also keeping my body clear of the ball, particularly in 40 and 41. I don't want to be too close to the ball. Having

36

37

38

45

39

40

46

41

gone down and played the stroke I haven't jerked myself away immediately after. The ball is coming off the side wall and if it is not hitting the nick then it is going to go very close, making a very awkward return for my opponent. I always try and make sure that I go through with the stroke. There is a tendency for the average player to let the racket drop at impact, to uncock the wrist and so flick at the ball rather than stroke it into the corner. A flick automatically means one loses control over the ball and there is far greater likelihood of the ball being scooped up on the front wall leaving your opponent with a sitter to put away.

47

BACKHAND DROP

This is my favourite stroke and here I am able to play it in an ideal position from near the short line. I have made a comfortable approach to the ball and the racket positions, 42–44, are ideal for early preparation. I gradually bring the racket back to its highest position, 48, and my feet are nicely in line and well balanced as I begin the stroke. You can clearly see I am transferring my weight on to the front foot for production of the stroke in 45–48, and because the ball is coming through low I have had to bend my knees and my back. The racket head becomes obviously open in 49 and from

42

43

44

45

46

47

48

49

50

52

there on to the end, note, the racket face is seen to be open. I hit the ball well away from the leading foot, 50, 51, and a little in front of the left foot. Tremendous emphasis is placed on the bending of the legs. My left arm is solidly planted and there is no overreaching or overbalancing. Impact is at 50. After impact through 52 the follow-through is slight. I keep my head down, my eyes follow the ball, there is no sudden twisting of the body, and finally, 53, I can start to adjust my weight and move back towards a position just near to the T (54).

51

53

52

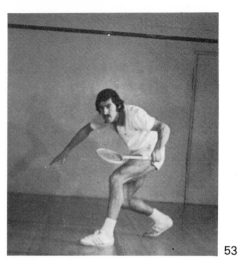

53

54

54

There is one – just one – free shot in squash and that is the service. It is the only stroke you play when you have all the advantages, so force the pace. No matter how good your opponent is, he has to stand at the back of the court to receive service. (see photo D on page 67). Be aggressive and always positive.

To serve an outright winner is exceedingly difficult but at worst the opponent will be placed under pressure. Hit the ball high on the front wall – just off centre, midway between the cut line and the top red line – so that it will float back to the

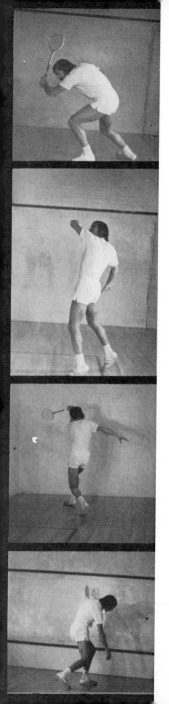

side wall. That will make your opponent either scramble a high volley away from the wall or, better still, let the ball go into the backhand corner. From in there, he may have difficulty in returning the serve.

Vary your serve from time to time. After innumerable high floaters toss over a hard-hit serve straight at him. See how quickly he moves.

Don't forget, if you are right-handed and playing a leftie, like me, to attack him on his backhand. I often notice right-handers continuing to serve to a leftie's forehand as though they haven't noticed that he is left-handed.

From the right box I like a simple forehand volley lob serve, played with my right foot forward and my left anchored in the box. From the left box I often use the same forehand lob serve. It leaves me with my back to my opponent so I usually sneak a look at him out of the corner of my eye just as I start my backswing. Keep your swing smooth. A tennis serve will set you spinning like a top and allow your opponent to kill the ball before you can focus your whirling eyes on it.

RETURN OF SERVICE

When returning service, your main aim should be to place the ball as far away from your opponent as possible, so only occasionally play the ball short. Instead hit the ball as high as possible to the back corners – either straight down the side wall or high across court.

The correct position to take up to return service is about one foot behind the outside back corner of the service box. From this position you will be able to take the ball on the volley or you will be able to move backwards to play the ball off the back wall if necessary.

Remember, you are the receiver now, the man momentarily in the position of weakness, so be judicious and compromise. You should try and aim your returns at the back corners of the court to drag your opponent away from the centre. Then you can take over the T and dominate him.

57

4. How To Win

Jonah, I'm playing an arch rival in the semi-finals of the club championship tomorrow night. We have played each other many times so we know each other's game. We are about the same standard. How can I make sure that I beat him tomorrow night?

First, think positively. Remember the games you have won against him and not those you have lost. Be realistic. You know that the game you like to play is a game he likes to play also, so you will have to be at your best to beat him. That means cutting out mistakes, playing percentage squash.

Second, use the knock-up not as a formality but as the priceless opportunity it really is to get the feel of the ball. Don't try and hit too hard too soon. Get your swing into a groove on both the forehand and backhand. You know that he normally volleys well, but this time toss up a lob or two and see how he responds. It may be that his timing is off tonight. On the other hand, if he hits it tremendously hard into the nick then you know what shot not to play.

Third, prepare yourself for the court. Note the speed of the ball. Is it coming off the front wall faster or slower than usual? Remind yourself of the height of the ceilings, fling one high into the lights to see what sort of lighting there is. Get all this done during the knock-up. When you come to spinning the racket you are prepared for battle. So far you have just been sounding him out.

I lose the serve, Jonah. How do I start?

Pretend the first point is match point. You must have seen people playing feverishly later on in a game when they want those crucial points. They should have been playing that way from the start. You're out of hand so you want to get the service back. You're looking for length immediately, trying to push him to the back of the court so that you can then pull him to the front. Don't change the speed of a rally too soon. Don't yet go for that cross-court volley nick you've been practising. You haven't got your rhythm. Start sensibly and fight for every ball.

Nevertheless I make a bad start, Jonah. I've lost the first game. He went through me much faster than I anticipated and I am a little worried. What do I do now?

You lost it because he got in quickly, got a rhythm going. You were a bit nervy, couldn't find a length, made some unforced errors. You've got to get your rhythm and get the ball to the back of

the court so that by forcing your way into a rally you can get a feel of the game. Don't be hustled. If you want to, pause for a moment before serving. Take an extra deep breath after the end of a rally as you walk into the service box. Above all play positively. Don't throw away this game with a flurry of shots off the top of your head.

If you find you are being blasted off court remember to hit the ball a little higher on the front wall, and play some lobs to break his pace and rhythm. This will prevent your opponent from having such easy targets around half court. Don't worry about losing that first game. The bloke's still got to win two more and you know that your percentage game will work, given time. Keep cool.

I was better in that game, Jonah. I got him off the T and back into the corners by hitting the ball higher as you suggested. But I still lost the game 9–5. Two–love down, what about the crucial third?

Play for time. Don't despair, because the third game is paradoxically the hardest game for him to win – subconsciously he feels he is almost home and so he relaxes. I played Geoff Hunt and lost the first game 9–3 and the second by the same margin. I was 7–0 down in the third, about as near to defeat as I could get without actually losing. Then he tried some risky shots and I crept back, 1–7, 2–7, 3–7 until I won the game 9–7. I didn't lose faith in myself. I was fighting for my life, like a rat in a trap. As long as you are playing good basic sound squash he will make a couple of errors as he gets anxious to finish you off. Even if you lose 3–0 you must make him win every point in that third game. Pressure him slightly, force him further back in the court. Unless you are completely outclassed in the first two games then you will probably win the third. It's odd the way that happens but, believe me, it usually does. I've had it happen to me often enough.

Fine, Jonah, I win that game 9–4. I win the fourth too, but now I'm very tired. I've had a hard day in the office. The blister on my right hand is hurting like hell and I've had to fight all the way to get back into the game.

Stop complaining. This is mental this game. This is where you show your character. You have to concentrate more than ever. Now it's your turn to make sure that having regained supremacy you don't throw it away. Never hurry. Keep calm. Keep it simple. As your legs ache, your arm hurts, your blister bursts and oozes

61

muck all over your hand, as all this happens think to yourself that it was you not he who clawed your way back from the abyss. And if you can do that then you can hold on for one more game. I always say that the start of the fifth is the start of a new match. You've come back on a radar beam to win the last two games but there is no easy way to win the fifth. You are getting more confident now, which is right. But don't forget you haven't won yet. You have just made it even steven.

It's scrappy squash, Jonah, with neither of us able to take a decent lead. Now it's 8–8 in the fifth.

At this point special tactics are called for. I don't reveal these to everyone. First you hit him with a left hook. Then you trip him with your racket. If that doesn't work, John, then start praying. Seriously, now you must not snatch at a ball. Don't rush a shot, don't crash a drive, don't attempt a delicate drop. Your heart is beating faster, your breathing is harder, everything is mitigating against delicacy.

You've gone to 8–8 in the fifth. You've worked for an hour and fifteen minutes. Why throw it away by planting the ball straight into the tin when going for a cross-court volley? Why not a straight one instead? Greatness comes out when

62

a player is absolutely shagged yet he still plays the percentage game. At 8–8 Cam Nancarrow would try for a nick from a return of service. He would probably get it too. But that's Cam Nancarrow. For the average person I say no, don't do that. Stick with the basic, tidy, unfrilly squash that has got you to 8–8. And, John?

Yes, Jonah?

Stop complaining about your hand, your breath, your feet, your legs and your racket.

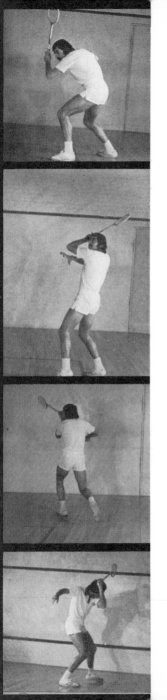

5. Problem Situations – What Do I Do Now?

A My opponent is well balanced on the T. He has drawn me up to the front forehand corner. How do I hit the ball without hitting him, Jonah, or without hitting it to him?

Answer: By lobbing straight down the nearest side wall or high across court, John. You could try a hard-hit cross-court drive.

A

B My opponent is on the T looking like a giant octopus. I am penned in the back corner. How do I get the ball out so that I have time to get out of the corner myself and can regain the initiative?

Answer: Again you must hit the ball high down the side wall, John, or high across court. But really high this time. Another possibility is a slow boast, which will take him to the front of the court where he will have to wait for the ball to land and that will give you time to come out of the corner.

B

65

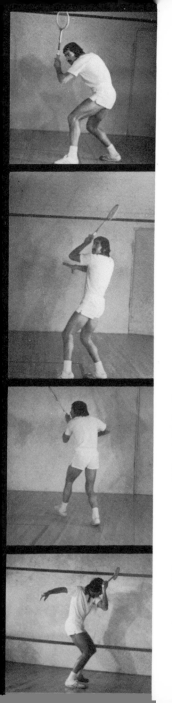

C My opponent is right by my side at half court. How do I get him out of the way? We keep barging one another and it is getting very frustrating.

Answer: A hard drive, aimed just off centre to force him backwards to three-quarter court. Or: a reverse angle played across his body up to the front of the court. But beware of the penalty point or let in this situation.

C

D My opponent, a big, strong-armed man, constantly hurls down fast winning serves. How do I overcome them?

Answer: Do not stare at the front wall. The answer is not written there. Watch him and the ball whenever possible. Make sure your feet are properly aligned and turn your head to watch him. Don't stand too near the side wall, nor too far back.

D

E My opponent's deep drives have me in trouble in the back corners. I am afraid to go in and hit for fear of breaking my racket. Besides, I feel there is not enough room there for me to swing at the ball. What do I do now, Jonah?

Answer: A possibility is a back wall boast – hit the ball upwards on to the back wall and hope that it will carry back on to the front wall. Or try a slow high boast, as in **B**. Or shorten the grip on the racket, as Gogi Alauddin does in such situations, and hope to squeeze it out.

E

F My opponent's high serves just kiss the side wall. I rush forward to try and volley them, miss and by the time I have recovered the ball is past me and dying in the back corner. Help!

Answer: Move further forward, John. Threaten the server. Then you will be able to try and volley the ball before it hits the side wall and if you miss that shot then you have a second chance – when it comes off the side wall.

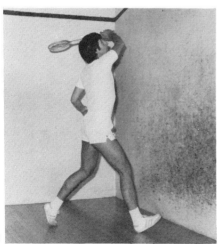

F

69

6. Joining A Club

I am anxious to play more, Jonah, but when I tried to join my local club I couldn't get in. Membership was closed they said. I rang some of the other clubs in my area but they were all full too.

I hope you put your name down on a waiting list for one of them, John. Meantime, isn't there a sports centre in your area? Most people in England have one within twenty-five miles, according to the Sports Council. You will find a heavy demand for courts there too. But the advantage of these centres is that you don't have to be a member. You can just ring up, book a court, pay your money and then play. Consequently this form of squash is quite cheap.

I'll do that but I would still like to join a club. How much will it cost me do you think?

Depends how long the waiting list is. It won't be cheap and over a year it will certainly cost you more than at your local sports centre. Annual membership might be as much as £20, probably nearer £30 if you live in London, and court fees could be anything up to 75p an hour for a half hour per person.

And how do I get some lessons?

The sports centre might well have a professional or amateur coach visiting on certain nights each week. Enquire at reception. I think you are doing the right thing if you want to join a club to get competitive squash. You will be able to play against the better club players and if you are good enough – when you are good enough – you will be able to play in club matches. Sports centres are excellent for those who just want to thrash around for exercise with a regular partner. But for competition, it's got to be a club.

You may be lucky enough to find a sports centre which runs club teams as well.

7. Training

After more than ten years and thousands of miles of running I consider myself a bit of an expert on training. Rest assured, however, I am not going to prescribe anything like my daily schedule for you.

As I see it the main problem for the average player is finding the time. I would think that most amateurs can manage a maximum of five hours each week in which to play and very few would want to give up any of that time to go running as well. So I shall try and outline a way for people with limited time to train and play whilst continuing to enjoy their squash.

First of all, try and get games with players who are better than you are. You will learn so much from them. Most important, you will be under pressure. Everything will seem to happen a half-second faster, but by learning to cope with a more hectic pace you will get better. Secondly, take lessons if you can. A coach should be able to pinpoint any obvious weaknesses, such as incorrect grip, and help to iron them out of your game. Thirdly, practise by yourself. Now I know this sounds very boring – and believe me I should know, after having done it for years – but it can be interesting if you know what to do instead of simply aimlessly hitting a ball

72

around court. Half an hour each week practising alone should be enough for you soon to notice an improvement.

How many times can you hit a ball down the forehand or backhand side wall without it catching the side wall and bouncing back into mid-court? Can you stand on the T and play a drop shot into either the forehand or backhand front corners? If you can't hit a drop standing still what chance do you have when you are running? Can you hit ten successive volleys forehand and backhand on to the front wall? Better still, can you hit ten forehand and ten backhand volleys?

Another simple exercise is this: stand deep in a court on either the forehand or backhand side and hit a boast. Run up to the front and as the ball ricochets off the front wall hit a straight drive so the ball heads back down the side wall. If you boasted from the forehand corner it will be a backhand drive; if you boasted from the backhand corner then it will be a forehand drive. This will help improve your boasts and also sharpen up your footwork on your drives. If you are feeling really tigerish then see how long you can last by doing this exercise non-stop.

For variation, and to make the practice a physical one as well, do some ghosting to work the heart and lungs. Ghosting is the vile training I devised some years ago,

73

simply moving around court as in a game, sprinting to the front to play a drop, stretching to the back and leaping for a volley. The difference is that you have no opponent and no ball when you ghost. Nevertheless, pretend it is a game and if you do this hard you will find at first that a minute or so is hard work.

That's all. I did say, didn't I, that I want to provide you with a way of improving without interfering too much with your living.

8. Doubles

The doubles game of squash is an extremely enjoyable game. But I have a number of conditions that I would want satisfied before I ventured on court. By the way, the size of a doubles court is approximately half as big again (45 ft/13·72 m by 25 ft/7·62 m) as a singles court. You need a bouncier, harder ball to play with, too. To the best of my knowledge there are only a handful of doubles courts in Britain. Consequently 99% of all doubles games are played on singles courts.

I carry a torch for doubles because I think a proper doubles gives a player as much opportunity to think out his strokes as a proper singles; maybe more because the pressure of having two extra people on court is greater.

I should like to see the development of a new hybrid court: one of the existing 32 ft/9·75 m length of a singles court, but six to eight feet (two to two and a half metres) wider. I would use the existing ball. Such a court would be a good commercial proposition because the overheads of a doubles court are no greater than a singles court and four players can use it at once.

But that is by the way. As a game doubles is tremendously good fun for

75

older players who can get a sense of out-manoeuvring their rivals in a series of strokes without the frenetic physical activity necessary in singles. Doubles can be terribly skilful, fast and exciting to watch. A few years ago I played in a pro doubles tournament at Walton-on-Thames and the galleries were packed each night. Not only because there was a possibility of one of us getting a racket in our face, either.

Here I come to my first condition. I will not play doubles with anyone whom I have not seen play before. I value my head, arms, shoulders, even my ugly mug enough not to put them at the mercy of a bloke with a scything follow-through on the forehand.

My second condition is this. The game must not be allowed to become so serious that a player is tempted to play a stroke when his better judgement suggests he should take a let. To my mind, the only way to play doubles on a singles court and, to a lesser degree a full-size court, is on the understanding that a let is always taken in preference to a shot. It is avoiding injury again.

Scoring at doubles is slightly different. It is like American scoring in that every point won by either side is a point added to their total; instead of merely earning them the right to serve as in singles. A

76

good thing about serving in doubles is that a double fault in singles – serving out of court, for instance – is only a single fault in doubles. I think that is good because it encourages players to attack with the service.

9. Refereeing

Nearly every club player will be aware that he or she probably does not know the rules too well. The rule about fair view and freedom of stroke is one that most club players probably don't fully understand. There is no disgrace in that. Many top-class players don't understand it either. At club level this ignorance of the rule often causes players to get in each other's way, just as they do at the game's highest level, though sometimes here it is deliberate.

The fact is, and take this as a simple guide to players and referees, that a player, having hit a stroke must then make every effort to clear out of the way. In clubs there are the half-court men, who linger around the middle of the court as if they want to buy that plot of land. Practically nothing will move them from their blessed position.

There are those who play a drop shot and then don't move away at all. They remain with their heads down, their bottoms sticking out admiring their shot. And if their opponent has to ask for a let to avoid having to run around them they feel cheated. They are present in every club in the land.

Then there are those big swingers, the men who wield their rackets as if they were throwing the hammer – enormous backswings on the forehand; long follow-throughs on the backhand.

If you have to play such a chap in your club competition the first thing to do is politely to ask him whether he would mind having a referee. If he does mind it's probably because he feels guilty and you will have to insist on one.

If you play regular competitions at your club, or if you play in the leagues, then you will come across this chap frequently. You might be prepared to risk playing him, however. On the other hand, you might be very gentlemanly, and simply politely decline to play him.

With the man who stares at the front wall you might try giving him a rap in the back as you go past just to remind him that he is in your way. But that is a fairly drastic measure. He might thump you back. It is probably better in the long run to get a referee or just to give him a miss.

As a piece of general advice for club players who are asked to referee I would insist that they first read the rules. That said they then have to rely on their common sense when they come to referee-ing. They must not assume delusions of grandeur the moment they have the power to award penalty points. I would advise almost the opposite to an inexperienced referee. I would also say that

79

club referees must realize that if there is any doubt in their minds then they ought to give a let. If, in other words, they have to think for a few seconds before pronouncing then it is probably better for them to give a let.

10. The Rules

These Rules were approved by the International Squash Rackets Federation, the game's world-wide governing body, in 1976 and became effective on 1st January 1977.

1. THE GAME

HOW PLAYED. The game of Squash Rackets is played between two players with standard rackets, with balls officially approved by I.S.R.F. and in a rectangular court of standard dimensions, enclosed on all four sides.

2. THE SCORE

A match shall consist of the best of three or five games at the option of the promoters of the competition. Each game is 9 points up; that is to say, the player who first wins 9 points wins the game, except that, on the score being called 8-all for the first time, Hand-out may choose, before the next service is delivered, to continue the game to 10, in which case the player who first scores two more points, wins the game. Hand-out must in either case clearly indicate his choice to the Marker, if any, and to his opponent.

81

Note to Referees. If Hand-out does not make clear his choice before the next service, the Referee shall stop play and require him to do so.

3. POINTS

HOW SCORED. Points can only be scored by Hand-in. When a player fails to serve or to make a good return in accordance with the rules, the opponent wins the stroke. When Hand-in wins a stroke, he scores a point; when Hand-out wins a stroke, he becomes Hand-in.

4. THE RIGHT TO SERVE

The right to serve first is decided by the spin of a racket. Thereafter the server continues to serve until he loses a stroke, when his opponent becomes the server, and so on throughout the match.

5. SERVICE

The ball before being struck shall be thrown in the air and shall not touch the walls or floor. The ball shall be served on to the front wall, so that on its return, unless volleyed, it would fall to the floor in the back quarter of the court opposite to the server's box from which the service has been delivered.

82

At the beginning of each game and of each hand, the server may serve from either box, but after scoring a point he shall then serve from the other, and so on alternately as long as he remains Hand-in or until the end of the game If the server serves from the wrong box, there shall be no penalty and the service shall count as if served from the correct box, except that the Hand-out may, if he does not attempt to take the service, demand that it be served from the other box.

A player with the use of only one arm may utilize his racket to project the ball into the air.

6. GOOD SERVICE

A service is good which is not a fault or which does not result in the server serving his hand-out in accordance with Rule 9. If the server serves one fault, he shall serve again.

7. FAULT

A service is a fault (unless the server serves his hand-out under Rule 9.):

a. If the server fails to stand with one foot on the floor at least within and not touching the line surrounding the service box at the moment of striking the ball (called a foot-fault).

83

b.   If the ball is served on to, or below, the cut line.

c.   If the ball served first touches the floor on, or in front of, the short line.

d.   If the ball served first touches the floor in the wrong quarter of the court as that from which it was served or on the half-court line. (The wrong quarter of the court is the rear left for a service from the left-hand box, and the rear right for a service from the right-hand box).

8. FAULT, IF TAKEN

Hand-out may take a fault, If he attempts to do so, the service thereupon becomes good and the ball continues in play. If he does not attempt to do so, the ball shall cease to be in play, provided that, if the ball, before it bounces twice upon the floor, touches the server or anything he wears or carries, the server shall lose the stroke.

9. SERVING HAND-OUT

The server serves his Hand-out and loses the stroke:

a.   If the ball is served on to, or below, the board, or out of court, or against any part of the court before the front wall.

b.   If the ball is not thrown in the air, or

touches the wall or floor before being struck, or if he fails to strike the ball, or strikes it more than once.

c.   If he serves two consecutive faults.

d.   If the ball, before it has bounced twice upon the floor, or has been struck by his opponent, touches the server or anything he wears or carries.

10. LET

A let is an undecided stroke, and the service or rally, in respect of which a let is allowed, shall not count and the server shall serve again from the same box. A let shall not annul a previous fault.

11. THE PLAY

After a good service has been delivered, the players return the ball alternately until one or other fails to make a good return, or the ball otherwise ceases to be in play in accordance with the rules.

12. GOOD RETURN

A return is good if the ball, before it has bounced twice upon the floor, is returned by the striker on to the front wall above the board, without touching the floor or any part of the striker's body or clothing, provided the ball is not hit twice or out of court.

85

Note to Referees. It shall not be considered a good return if the ball touches the board before or after it hits the front wall.

13. STROKES

HOW WON. A player wins a stroke:
a.   Under Rule 9.
b.   If he opponent fails to make a good return of the ball in play.
c.   If the ball in play touches his opponent or anything he wears or carries, except as is otherwise provided by Rules 14 and 15.
d.   If a stroke is awarded by the Referee as provided for in the Rules.

14. HITTING AN OPPONENT WITH THE BALL

If an otherwise good return of the ball has been made, but before reaching the front wall it hits the striker's opponent, or his racket, or anything he wears or carries, then:

a.   If the ball would have made a good return, and would have struck the front wall without first touching any other wall, the striker shall win the stroke, except that, if the striker shall have followed the ball round, and so turned, before playing the ball, a let shall be allowed.
b.   If the ball would otherwise have made

a good return, a let shall be allowed.

c. If the ball would not have made a good return, the striker shall lose the stroke. The ball shall cease to be in play, even if it subsequently goes up.

15. FURTHER ATTEMPTS TO HIT THE BALL

If the striker strikes at, and misses the ball he may make further attempts to return it. If, after being missed, the ball touches his opponent, of his racket, or anything he wears or carries, then:

a. If the striker would otherwise have made a good return, a let shall be allowed.
b. If the striker could not have made a good return, he loses the stroke.

If any such further attempt is successful, but the ball, before reaching the front wall, hits the striker's opponent, or his racket, or anything he wears or carries, a let shall be allowed, and Rule 14 a shall not apply.

16. APPEALS

1 An appeal may be made against any decision of the Marker, except for 2 a and b below.
2 a. No appeal shall be made in respect of foot-faults.

b. No appeal shall be made in respect of the Marker's call of 'fault' to the first service.

c. If the Marker calls 'fault' to the second service, the server may appeal, and if the decision is reversed, a let shall be allowed.

d. If the Marker allows the second service, Hand-out may appeal, either immediately, or at the end of the rally, if he has played the ball, and if the decision is reversed, Hand-in becomes Hand-out.

e. If the Marker does not call 'fault' to the first service, Hand-out may appeal that the service was a fault, provided he makes no attempt to play the ball. If the Marker does not call 'Out' or 'Not Up' to the first service, Hand-out may appeal, either immediately or at the end of the rally, if he has played the ball. In either case, if the appeal is disallowed, Hand-out shall lose the stroke.

3 An appeal under Rule 12. shall be made at the end of the rally.

4 In all cases where an appeal for a let is desired, this appeal shall be made by addressing the Referee with the words 'Let, please'. Play shall thereupon cease until the Referee has given his decision.

5 No appeal may be made after the delivery of a service for anything that occurred before that service was delivered.

17. FAIR VIEW AND FREEDOM TO PLAY THE BALL

a. After playing a ball, a player must make every effort to get out of his opponent's way. That is:

i) A player must make every effort to give his opponent a fair view of the ball, so that he may sight it adequately for the purpose of playing it.

ii) A player must make every effort not to interfere with, or crowd, his opponent in the latter's attempt to get to, or play, the ball.

iii) A player must make every effort to allow his opponent, as far as the latter's position permits, freedom to play the ball directly to the front wall, or side walls near the front wall.

b. If any such form of interference has occurred, and, in the opinion of the Referee, the player has not made every effort to avoid causing it, the Referee shall on appeal, or without waiting for an appeal, award the stroke to his opponent.

c. However, if interference has occurred, but in the opinion of the Referee the

89

BACKHAND DROP

BACKHAND VOLLEY

BACKHAND BOAST

BACKHAND DRIVE

player has made every effort to avoid causing it, the Referee shall, on appeal, or may without waiting for an appeal, award a let, except that if his opponent is prevented from making a winning return by such interference or by distraction from the player, the Referee shall award the stroke to the opponent.

d. When, in the opinion of the Referee, a player refrains from playing the ball, which, if played, would clearly and undoubtedly have won the rally under the terms of Rule 14 a, he shall be awarded the stroke.

Notes to Referees

a. The practice of impeding an opponent in his efforts to play the ball by crowding or obscuring his view, is highly detrimental to the game, and Referees should have no hesitation in enforcing paragraph b above.

b. The words 'interfere with' in a(ii) above must be interpreted to include the case of a player having to wait for an excessive swing of his opponent's racket.

18. LET, WHEN ALLOWED

Notwithstanding anything contained in these rules, and provided always that the striker could have made a good return:

1 A Let may be allowed:
  a. If, owing to the position of the

90

striker, his opponent is unable to avoid being touched by the ball before the return is made.

Note to Referees This rule shall be construed to include the cases of the striker, whose position in front of his opponent makes it impossible for the latter to see the ball, or who shapes as if to play the ball and changes his mind at the last moment, preferring to take the ball off the back wall, the ball in either case hitting his opponent, who is between the striker and the back wall. This is not, however, to be taken as conflicting in any way with the Referee's duties under Rule 17.

b. If the ball in play touches any articles lying in the court.
c. If the striker refrains from hitting the ball owing to a reasonable fear of injuring his opponent.
d. If the striker, in the act of playing the ball, touches his opponent.
e. If the Referee is asked to decide an appeal and is unable to do so.
f. If a player drops his racket, calls out or in any other way distracts his opponent, and the Referee considers that such occurrence has caused the opponent to lose the stroke.

2 A Let shall be allowed:
a. If Hand-out is not ready and does

not attempt to take the service.
b. If a ball breaks during play.
c. If an otherwise good return has been made, but the ball goes out of court on its first bounce.
d. As provided for in Rules 14, 15, 16.2 c, 23 and 24.

3   Provided always that no let shall be allowed in respect of any attempt which a player makes to play the ball, except as provided for under Rules 18.1 d, 18.2 b and c, and 15.

4   Unless an appeal is made by one of the players, no let shall be allowed except where these rules definitely provide for a let, namely Rules 14 a, 14 b, 17 and 18.2 b, 18.2 c.

19. NEW BALL

At any time, when the ball is not in actual play, a new ball may be substituted by mutual consent of the players, or on appeal by either player at the discretion of the Referee.

20. KNOCK-UP

1   The Referee shall allow on the court of play to either player, or to the two players together, a period not exceeding five minutes immediately preceding the

start of play for the purpose of knocking-up. In the event of a separate knock-up, the choice of knocking-up first shall be decided by the spin of a racket. The Referee shall allow a further period for the players to warm the ball up if the match is being resumed after a considerable delay.

2   Where a new ball has been substituted under Rule 18.2 b or 19, the Referee shall allow the ball to be knocked up to playing condition. Play shall resume on the direction of the Referee, or prior mutual consent of the players.

3   The ball shall remain on the court in view between games. Except by mutual consent of the players, knocking-up is not permitted between games.

21. PLAY IN A MATCH IS TO BE CONTINUOUS

After the first service is delivered, play shall be continuous so far as is practical, provided that:

1   At any time play may be suspended owing to bad light or other circumstances beyond the control of the players, for such period as the Referee shall decide. In the event of play being suspended for the day, the match shall start afresh, unless both players agree to the contrary.

2   The Referee may award a game to the opponent of any player, who, in his opinion, persists, after due warning, in delaying the play in order to recover his strength or wind, or for any other reason.

3   An interval of one minute shall be permitted between games and of two minutes between the fourth and fifth games of a five-game match. A player may leave the court during such intervals, but shall be ready to resume play at the end of the stated time. When ten seconds of the interval permitted between games are left, the Marker shall call 'Ten seconds' to warn the players to be ready to resume play. Should either player fail to do so when required by the Referee, a game may be awarded to his opponent.

4   In the event of an injury, the Referee may require a player to continue play or concede the match, except where the injury is contributed to by his opponent, or where it was caused by dangerous play on the part of the opponent. In the former case, the Referee may allow time for the injured player to receive attention and recover, and in the latter, the injured player shall be awarded the match under Rule 24.3 b.

5   In the event of a ball breaking, a new ball may be knocked up, as provided for in Rule 20.2.

Notes to Referees

a. In allowing time for a player to receive attention and recover, the Referee should ensure that there is no conflicting with the obligation of a player to comply with Rule 21.2, that is, that the effects of the injury are not exaggerated and used as an excuse to recover strength or wind.

b. The Referee should not interpret the words 'contributed to' by the opponent to include the situation where the injury to the player is a result of that player occupying an unnecessarily close position to his opponent.

22. CONTROL OF A MATCH

A match is normally controlled by a Referee, assisted by a Marker. One person may be appointed to carry out the functions of both Referee and Marker. When a decision had been made by a Referee, he shall announce it to the players.

Up to one hour before the commencement of a match either player may request a Referee or Marker other than appointed, and this request may be considered and a substitute appointed. Players are not permitted to request any such change after the commencement of a match, unless both agree to do so. In either case the decision as to whether an official is to be replaced or not must remain in the hands of the Tournament Referee, where applicable.

23. DUTIES OF MARKER

1 The Marker calls the play and the score, with the server's score first. He shall call 'Fault', 'Foot-fault', 'Out' or 'Not up' as appropriate.

2 If in the course of play, the Marker calls 'Not up' or 'Out', or 'Fault' or 'Foot-fault' to a second service, the rally shall cease.

3 If the Marker's decision is reversed on appeal, a let shall be allowed, except as provided for in Rule 24 d and e.

4 Any service or return shall be considered good unless otherwise called.

5 After the server has served a fault, which has not been taken, the Marker shall repeat the score and add the words 'One fault', before the server serves again. This call should be repeated should subsequent rallies end in a let, until the point is finally decided.

6 When no Referee is appointed, the Marker shall exercise all the powers of the Referee.

7 If the Marker is unsighted or uncertain he shall call on the Referee to make the relevent decision; if the latter is unable to do so, a let shall be allowed.

24. DUTIES OF REFEREE

1 The Referee shall award Lets and Strokes and make decisions where called for by the rules, and shall decide all appeals, including those against the Marker's calls and decisions.

2 He shall in no way intervene in the Marker's calling except:

   a. Upon appeal by one of the players.
   b. As provided for in Rule 17.
   c. When it is evident that the score has been incorrectly called, in which case he should draw the Marker's attention to the fact.
   d. When the Marker has failed to call the ball 'Not up' or 'Out', and on appeal he rules that such was in fact the case, the stroke should be awarded accordingly.
   e. When the Marker has called 'Not up' or 'Out', and on appeal he rules that this was not the case, a Let shall be allowed except that if in the Referee's opinion, the Marker's call had interrupted an undoubted winning return, he shall award the stroke accordingly.
   f. The Referee is responsible that all times laid down in the rules are strictly adhered to.

3 In exceptional cases, the Referee may order:

a. A player, who has left the court, to play on.
b. A player to leave the court and to award the match to the opponent.
c. A match to be awarded to a player whose opponent fails to be present in court within ten minutes of the advertised time of play.
d. Play to be stopped in order to warn that the conduct of one or both of the players is leading to an infringement of the rules. A Referee should avail himself of this rule as early as possible when either player is showing a tendency to break the provisions of Rule 17.
e. If after a warning a player continues to contravene Rule 20.3 then the Referee may award a game to the opponent.

25. COLOUR OF PLAYERS' CLOTHING

For amateur events under the control of the I.S.R.F. players are required to wear all-white clothing. Member countries of the I.S.R.F. may legislate, if they so desire, to allow clothing of a light pastel colour to be worn for all other events under their control. (Note: Footwear is deemed clothing for this rule). The Referee's decision thereon to be final.

BOARD   The expression denoting a band, the top edge of which is 19 inches (0·483 m) from the floor across the lower part of the front wall above which the ball must be returned before the stroke is good.

CUT LINE   A line set out upon the front wall, the top edge of which is 6 feet (1·829 m) above the floor and extending the full width of the court.

N.B. All lines in the court should be 2″ (50 mm) wide, and should be red.

GAME BALL   The state of the game when the server requires one point to win is said to be 'Game Ball'.

HALF-COURT LINE   A line set out upon the floor parallel to the side walls, dividing the back half of the court into two equal parts.

HAND-IN   The player who serves.

HAND-OUT   The player who receives the service; also the expression used to indicate that Hand-in has become Hand-out.

HAND   The period from the time when a player becomes Hand-in until he becomes Hand-out.

MATCH BALL   The state of the match when the server requires one point to win is said to be 'Match Ball'.

NOT UP   The expression used to denote that a ball has not been served or returned above the board in accordance with the rules.

OUT   The ball is out when it touches the front, sides or back of the court above the area prepared for play or passes over any cross bars or other part of the roof of the court. The lines delimiting such area, the lighting equipment and the roof are out of court.

POINT   A point is won by the player who is Hand-in and who wins a stroke.

QUARTER COURT   One part of the back half of the court which has been divided into two equal parts by the half-court line.

SERVICE BOX OR BOX   A delimited area in each half court from within which Hand-in serves.

SHORT LINE   A line set upon the floor parallel to and 18 feet (5·486 m) from the front wall and extending the full width of the court.

STRIKER   The player whose turn it is to play after the ball has hit the front wall.

STROKE   A stroke is won by the player whose opponent fails to serve or make a good return in accordance with the rules.

TIME OR STOP   Expression used by the Referee to stop play.

TIN   A strip of resonant material covering the lower part of the front wall between the Board and the floor.

Length 32 feet (9·75 m). Breadth 21 feet (6·40 m).

Height to upper edge of cut line on front wall 6 feet (1·83 m).

Height to lower edge of front-wall line 15 feet (4·57 m).

Height to lower edge of back-wall line 7 feet (2·13 m).

Distance to further edge of short line from front wall 18 feet (5·49 m).

Height to upper edge of board from ground 19 inches (0·48 m).

Thickness of board (flat or rounded at top) ¼ to 1 inch (12·5 to 25 mm).

Height of side-wall line: The diagonal line joining the front-wall line and the back-wall line.

The sevice boxes shall be entirely enclosed on three sides within the court by lines, the short line forming the side nearest to the front wall, the side wall bounding the fourth side.

The internal dimensions of the service boxes shall be 5 ft 3 in (1·601 m).

All dimensions in the court shall be measured, where practicable, from the junction of the floor and front wall.

The lines marking the boundaries of the court shall be 2 inches in width (5 cm).

In respect of the outer boundary lines on the walls, it is suggested that the plaster should be so shaped as to produce a concave channel along such lines.

The width of other painted lines shall not exceed 2 inches (5 cm).

APPENDIX III: DIMENSIONS OF A RACKET

The overall length shall not exceed 27 inches or 685 mm. The internal stringing area shall not exceed $8\frac{1}{2}$ inches or 215 mm in length by $7\frac{1}{4}$ inches or 184 mm in breadth and the framework of the head shall measure not more than $\frac{9}{16}$ inch or 14 mm across the face by $\frac{13}{16}$ inch or 20 mm deep.

The framework of the head shall be of wood. The handle shaft shall be made of wood, cane, metal or glass fibre. The grip and foundation may be made of any suitable material.

APPENDIX IV: SPECIFICATION FOR SQUASH RACKET BALLS

The ball must conform to the following:
1 It must weigh not less than 23·3 grammes and not more than 24·6 grammes (approximately 360–380 grains).

2   Its diameter must be not less than 39·5 mm and not more than 41·5 mm (approximately 1·56 to 1·63 inches).

3   It must have a surface finish which guarantees continuing correct rebound.

4   It must be of a type specifically approved for championship play by the International Squash Rackets Federation.

5   Compression Specification:

i) The ball is mounted in an apparatus and a load of 0·5 kgm is applied which deforms the ball slightly. Subsequent deformation in the test is measured from this datum.

ii) An additional load of 2·4 kgm is applied and this deforms the ball further. The deformation from the datum postion is recorded.

iii) The deformation obtained in (ii) should be between 3 and 7 mm for balls of playing properties acceptable to the I.S.R.F.

APPENDIX V: CONSTRUCTION OF A COURT (CHAMPIONSHIP STANDARD)

The front wall shall be constructed of concrete, brick or similar material with a near smooth concrete or plaster finish. The side and rear walls to be constructed of similar materials. The rear wall, for viewing purposes, can be constructed of glass or similar materials.

All walls shall be white or near white. The space below the board shall be white.

The floor shall be constructed of light coloured wooden boards which will run lengthwise and not across the court. The floor must be level (horizontal).

The board and the space below it to the floor and an area above the height of play on the back wall (if wall continues upwards) should be constructed of some resonant material.

The minimum clear height above the front wall playing surface to be 1·25 metres, giving a clear height from the court floor of 5·8 metres (19 feet).

The minimum clear height at 3·5 metres back from the front wall to be 6·4 metres above the floor (21 feet).

Where a flat ceiling is used the height set at 3·5 metres back should apply as a minimum.